Kanawha to Appomattox

An American Civil War Story

Vernon Schmid

Vernon Schmid

FOR MY FAMILY

Also by Vernon Schmid

FICTION
Seven Days of the Dog
Watie's Wolves
Jacob's Trail
Showdown at Chalk Creek
Code of the West
Death in Cuernavaca: Short Stories
Winterkill

POETRY
The Irish Poems
The Journey Toward
As Tentative as Flight (co-author)
Canonical Hours
Testament
Sleeping with Zapata
Hog Killers and Other Poems
Kissing Moctezuma's Serpent
Westering: New and Selected Poems, 1974-2004
Otium Sanctum: Poems for the Journey Toward
Kansas
Medicine Bundle

NONFICTION
Media and Methods for Your Church
Houlihans and Horse Sense
More Houlihans and Horse Sense
Cherokee Myth and Legend
The Radical Implications of the Eucharist
Divine Fire: Reflections on the Revelation to   *John*
Cherokee Mounted Rifles: Muster Rolls with Commentary
Feliciano and Lady Bird
Kansas Indian Home Guard
Kanawha to Antietam and Back

PLAYS
Between Eleven and Thursday
One Night in Daylight
The Hare with Many Friends
Five Who Knew Jesus

Preface

After a summer of teaching at Fort Lewis College in Durango, Colorado, I drove east on U.S. Highway 160 to the little town of Springfield in Baca County, Colorado. Arriving at a modest home on the outskirts of town, I parked my Ford truck and went to the back door. I knocked. A man answered.

"John Milton Amrine was my great-grandfather," I said.

He laughed and said, "Mine, too. Come in cousin."

We visited for a while about our family connections and then he showed me an old faded photograph of our great-grandfather arriving on the high plains of southwest Colorado with extended family, several wagons, horses, mules, and a cow. There they stood staring at the camera, the woman in bonnets and long dressed, the men in broad-brimmed hats.

My host, the late Charles Amrine, invited me to take a trip to the Springfield Cemetery. There was a cluster of gravestones engraved with my mother's family name near the gate. Largest among them carries the inscription *John Milton Amrine, Capt., 28th Ohio Volunteer Infantry.*

Next to his gravestone is one reading *Catherine Amrine, Wife.*

Having spent decades researching family history the Civil War period fascinated me. On my father's side of the family, a great uncle had served in the 3rd U.S. Cavalry and a great-great grandfather had been with the Ohio Volunteer Infantry. Both units were part of the Army of the West and under the leadership of William Tecumseh Sherman brought the south to its knees in the invasion of George and the subsequent march to the sea.

However, I had not known of John Milton Amrine's Civil War connections until that summer day in Colorado. Later my wife, Susan, and I would visit the Antietam Battlefield and stand where he stood at the bridge that would bear the name of his General Burnside.

This small treatise is an attempt to share struggle of the war through the eyes of the Second German Regiment, the 28th Ohio Volunteer Infantry.

Vernon Schmid
June 3, 2013

Colonel August Moor
Second German Regiment
28th Ohio Volunteer Infantry Regiment

1

There was little surprise in the Ohio German communities when the call came for men to help preserve the Union. One German regiment had already been mustered and left to join other Union troops. The 2nd German Ohio Regiment, formed May 12, 1861 was

3

officially named was the 28th Ohio Volunteer Infantry. Organized and trained at Camp Dennison, Ohio, June 10, they mustered July 6, 1861. Augustus Moor, owner of a Cincinnati beer garden and a veteran of the Second Seminole War and the Mexican War, was elected colonel.

The 28th Ohio Volunteer Infantry volunteers were recruited from German meeting and beer halls located throughout the city of Cincinnati and Hamilton County. However, there was a scattering of recruits came from other parts of Ohio.   After training at Camp Dennison, Ohio, they were activated on July 17 with orders to depart for western Virginian (now West Virginia). However, the soldiers were not the only persons heading for the front. An article in the Cincinnati Daily Gazette related the following story about our unit:

"Col. Moor of the Second German Regiment (28th O.V.I.), thought it would be good for the men to have clean shirts once in a while, so accordingly when he left Cincinnati, he took with him ten stalwart Teutonic maidens – one for each company – whom he commissioned as laundresses. When the regiment arrived in western Virginia, General   Rosecrans objected to the innovation in army practice and ordered the return of the patriotic females. They started home as soon as possible, and arrived [in Cincinnati] ... in charge of the chaplain of the regiment."

By July 31, the troops were opposite Point Pleasant, in what was then western Virginia. Crossing the Ohio River into Virginia on August 1, eight soldiers accidentally drowned. This may have been an ill omen of what was yet to come for the men of the 28th Ohio, since most lives lost throughout the regiment's service occurred on western Virginia soil.

Virginia's western counties had little in common with the populous and politically powerful section of the state east of the mountains. Opposed to secession, political leaders from the west distanced themselves from Virginia's decision to leave the Union. The rift was so great that the western counties seceded — from the rest of the state. West Virginia became the 35th state on June 20, 1863. By then, the state was in firm Federal control. However, Union military dominance wasn't always that certain.

Control of transportation arteries in northwest Virginia, including the Staunton-Parkersburg Turnpike (now US 250) and the Baltimore & Ohio Railroad, was the main military focus in 1861. The first land battle of the war broke out June 3, 1861, when Union troops under General George McClellan brushed aside Confederate resistance at Philippi. By July, the Confederates had established strongholds on and around Rich Mountain. Union troops under McClellan and General William

Rosecrans successfully attacked those positions July 11–14, forcing the Confederates to withdraw.

The 2nd German Regiment's first assignment was to lift the siege on the Union-held town of Spencer Court House, Roane County, Virginia. On August 14 the Ohioans successfully dispersed Confederate forces and relieved the garrison, losing one man wounded. They then continued their march to Buckhannon, where they joined with the army under Brigadier General Rosecrans. Fittingly, the 28th was assigned to the brigade under Colonel Robert L. McCook, the Cincinnatian who had been commander of the 1st German Regiment.

Concerned with the defense of the Shenandoah Valley and the Virginia & Tennessee and Virginia Central Railroads, Confederate President Jefferson Davis sent Robert E. Lee west to try to straighten out the situation. In his first field activity of the war, Lee could not get the job done. Friction between local Confederate commanders, poor weather, disease, rugged terrain and general bumbling thwarted Lee's attempt to drive the Federals from their bastion at Cheat Mountain Fort.

At about the same time, Union forces drove Confederates from their fortifications at Carnifex Ferry. Eventually the Southerners retired to Camp Allegheny on the present-day Virginia-West Virginia border. A Union attack there on Dec. 13, 1861, failed.

After the fighting and maneuvering in 1861, the area that would become West Virginia was in Union hands. Confederates mounted periodic raids and isolated actions but never seriously threatened again.

Vernon Schmid

J. Nep Roesler Sketch of the Battle of Carnifex Ferry, 1861

2

Rosecrans attacked a Confederate force camped near Carnifex Ferry, a strategic crossing on the Gauley River. On September 10, they assaulted the rebel works above the ferry. During this battle the 28th Ohio suffered its first casualties as it went into action behind Schneider's battery near the center of the Union line.

At 5 pm, Rosecrans personally ordered Colonel August Moor to lead the 28th toward the Confederate right flank. Accompanying them were detachments of the 13th Ohio Infantry and the 23rd Ohio infantry, who were ordered to take position on the extreme left of the Federal line.

It was a difficult trek over steep, rocky ground. The brigade reached their destination after nightfall. Due to the exhaustion and the darkness of the night, they were ordered to settle in for the evening in front of the enemy works.

As the men of the 28th fell back to an unexposed position, they began to receive rifle fire from their front left flank, killing and wounding several in their ranks. The Germans responded instantly with a volley that lit up the dense thicket. They kept up a constant fire for several minutes until the enemy fire was silenced.

To their surprise, Colonel Moor discovered their targets had not been Confederates, but soldiers of the 13th and 23rd Ohio regiments. Their "friendly" fire killed two and wounded twenty-nine of the 28th. To add to the debacle, Colonel Moor and his second-in-command, Lieutenant-Colonel Gottfried Becker, a veteran of the German Revolution of 1848, fell off a rock ledge and injured themselves so badly command of the regiment fell upon a captain. In its first two months of service, our 28th Ohio had lost more men to accidents than it lost to the enemy.

The regiment continued its duty in the New River valley of West Virginia spending a month at Camp Anderson. They then set up winter quarters at Gauley Bridge, located at the forks of the Kanawha River. During the next five months, Col. Moor thoroughly instructed and drilled our regiment in the art of war.

On May 2, 1862, they marched to Fayetteville, West Virginia, where they were formed into the 2nd brigade of Brigadier General Jacob D. Cox's 9th Kanawha Division. Colonel Augustus Moor was assigned command of the brigade and Lieutenant-Colonel Becker became acting commander of the 28th Ohio Infantry for the rest of the war.

During Cox's expedition against the Tennessee & Virginia Railroad, the regiment figured prominently in the Battle of Princeton, Virginia. An unsuccessful flank attack against the Confederate right cost the 28th Ohio five men killed, 10 wounded, and 12 captured or missing. However, the Germans performed admirably in the face of heavy enemy fire. General Cox later reported, "The conduct of my command has been everything I could desire."

Returning to Flat Top Mountain, they spent the

summer exposed to guerrilla warfare in the pro-Southern valley of the Blue Stone River. During service in the mountainous backcountry of West Virginia, the Ohioans often fought bushwhackers and irregulars including the famous McCoys of the coming Hatfield & McCoy feud. Before their terms of enlistment were complete, they would become known for their skill in the art of guerrilla tactics.

On August 25, 1862, the 28th Ohio was ordered to Washington, D.C., as part of Major General George McClellan's Army of the Potomac marching noth to head off Lee's march into Maryland. During the Sept. 14th Battle of South Mountain, Maryland, they lost 3 more killed and 12 wounded while pinned down in J. Martz's cornfield at Fox's Gap. But, that was only a harbinger of what was to become. The next stop was a place called Antietam where on 17 September the 28th suffered 22 casualties when it became the first regiment of the IX Corps to ford Antietam Creek above the infamous Burnside's Bridge. Their commander this point was a young Colonel George Crook.

After the war established the National Tribune. It carried many articles about the war and a large number of letters by veterans. One such letter was from a former colleague of General George Crook questioning what really happened at Burnside Bridge where Crook commanded the Kanawha Division. Crook answered the question. One of his company commanders, John Milton

Amrine, supported his statement.

Headquarters Department of the Platte Omaha Neb Dec 1867

John T Booth M D

My Dear Doctor On the morning of Sept 17 Col Christie of Gen Coxs staff came to me while we were lying in that sunken cornfield where you remember we passed the night and told me that Gen Sturgiss Division had failed to take the bridge or had been repulsed. I dont just recall the language now. Upon my Inquiring where the bridge was he replied Damned if I know but supposed it was in the direction he pointed. Upon my remonstrating against such an Indefinite order he repdled In a curt manner that he had done his duty in giving the order and it was my duty to obey it. Having heard the firing In the morning in the direction pointed out by Christie I went forward with the 11th Ohio to reconnolter. We had not proceeded far before we came across the dead and wounded of Gen Sturgiss Division. I went sufficiently far in advance to see the situation and to convince myself that the bridge could not be taken from that point I left the 11th Ohio where it was and took the 28th Ohio and a section of Simmonds Battery to the right of the 11th and up the creek into some small hills leaving the 3Cth (?) in the road near the brick house. I posted the section of artillery on a point that enfiladed

13

the enemys position and In the meantime had directed part of the 28th to cross the creek above the bridge by wading the stream keeping the remainder of the 28th as a support of the artillery.

My Intention was to cross the bridge with the 36th Ohio myself. In a short time after opening of the batterys fire and the crossing of the 28th above the position of the enemy they retreated and by the time I readied the 36th two regiments of some other command walked across the bridge without having anything to do with taking it. I may also add that these two regiments referred to were the first troops I saw outside of our own command. If any other troops than our brigade had anything to do with taking of the bridge I dont know It. I feel sure In my own mind they didn't.

Your sincerely Geo Crook

Crooks published statement received this support.

Editor National Tribune

About 830 the morning of Sept 17 1862 the 28th Ohio forming part of Gen George Crooks Brigade Kanawha Division Ninth Corps was ordered to take position about 150 yards to the right of Burnside Bridge at Antietam along the creek with directions to ford the stream as soon as Capt Simmons a Battery of 20 pounder Parrotts became engaged and assault the enemy. Pending the preparation of the regiment to execute this order Co B

*forming part of the support of Simmonss Battery was
directed to deploy as skirmishers to advance in the
direction of the bridge and feel the exact position of the
enemy. Immediately however as the skirmishers reached
the open ground a little to the northeast of the bridge
they became exposed to a fierce enfilading fire not only
from well posted sharpshooters but also from the main
force of the enemy posted on the hights and commanding
the* eastern approach to the bridge. *I, In command of Co
D being severely wounded and carried from the field left
the company In command of Lieut Grelf. Having located
the enemy Co B was withdrawn. The remainder of the
regiment had In the meantime forded the stream and
commenced advancing up the wood covered hight with
the enemy reluctantly and slowly falling back before
them. The regiment finally reached the crest of the hights
and held the position behind a stone fence until other
troops of the brigade Joined them when a further
advance was made Gen Crook in ordering the fording of
the creek permitted the passage of the bridge as stated in
the letter by Gen Crook which I append.*

John Amrine Captain Co D 28th Ohio and

Captain Veteran Reserve Corps Washington D C

Vernon Schmid

Great-

Burnside Bridge, Antietam Creek

**Grandfather John Milton Amrine's company forded the creek to right of
the bridge.**

Photo by Susan Schmid

28ᵗʰ Ohio Monument, Antietam

Photo by Susan Schmid

Plaque at Antietam
Photo by Susan Schmid

3

On October 14, the 28th headed back to West Virginia. Having broken away from the state of Virginia they were admitted to the Union as a state on June 20, 1863. For the next year, the 28th put their skill to work against guerilla units conducting frequent foraging and peacekeeping expeditions into the central and northern

regions of the state. They also constructed a fort at Beverly, West Virginia, to protect against rebel raiders. Hard marches over difficult Appalachian terrain, frequent skirmishes with Confederate home guard, and weeks of boredom in camp became the standard of everyday life for them.

Not until November 1863, did they return to heavy

combat. As part of Brigadier General William Averell's expedition into eastern West Virginia, Lieutenant Colonel Gottfried Becker skillfully led them in the crucial Battle of Droop Mountain on November 6, 1863.

Droop Mountain is located in the Greenbrier River Valley north of Lewisburg and is the site of West Virginia's last significant Civil War battle. The federal army of Brigadier General William W. Averell, made its second attempt to disrupt the Virginia-Tennessee Railroad at Salem, Virginia, faced again by the Confederate troops of Brigadier General John Echols.

Throughout the morning, Echols' smaller confederate army held the high ground and blocked the highway with artillery, but in the afternoon was overwhelmed by the crushing advance of federal infantry on his left flank. Following the collapse of his lines, Echols retreated south into Virginia with the remnants of his command. Federal Troops occupied Lewisburg on November 7, but being burdened with prisoners and captured livestock; General Averell elected to return to his headquarters in Beverly, West Virginia. There the army waited until early December when it mounted a third and ultimately successful attack on the vital railroad.

Operations in the Shenandoah Valley in the spring of 1864 drew remaining confederate troops out of west Virginia, thus leaving the new state securely under the control of the federal government for the remainder of the war.

The soldiers of the 28th displayed great gallantry under fire at the "Bloody Angle," where they helped to roll up the Confederate left flank and forced the enemy to flee from the field. In this battle, they lost 3 killed and 28 wounded, the second largest loss in Averell's army. Then the brigade returned to Beverly, West Virginia, to spend the winter of 1863-64.

Vernon Schmid

4

After returning from furlough on April 25, 1864, the 28th Ohio Infantry was formed into Colonel Moor's brigade of Major General Franz Sigel's Army of the Shenandoah. Five days later, Sigel marched his army south up the Shenandoah Valley from Martinsburg, West Virginia.

Brigadier General Jeremiah Sullivan, the division commander, assigned the 28th Ohio to guard the wagon trains positioned near Strasburg, Virginia. On May 15, as the Battle of New Market raged to the south, Confederate cavalry attacked five companies of the 28th Ohio at Strasburg. After a vicious fight, the 28th successfully drove off the rebels, but not before losing two men killed and ten captured. Meanwhile, the other five companies of the regiment aided the army's retreat from the New Market battlefield.

Following the New Market disaster, Major General David Hunter took command of the Army of the Shenandoah. At the end of May, the army was moving south again up the Valley. In a sad twist of fate, only eight days before most of the enlistments in the 28th Ohio were to expire, the regiment engaged in its bloodiest fight of the war.

On June 5, 1864, the 28th Ohio distinguished itself the Battle of Piedmont, Virginia. As part of Colonel August Moor's brigade holding the Union right, the Cincinnati Germans made two desperate charges against strongly defended Confederate works. Their attacks were turned back with great loss, losing five color-bearers in quick succession. A Confederate counterattack followed, and all of Moor's regiments retreated except for the 28th Ohio, which was left alone to fight six Confederate regiments. With the help of Union artillery fire, Becker's Germans single-handedly turned back the Rebel attack. Hunter ordered a third charge, and the soldiers of the 28th Ohio went bravely forward with their brigade. This time, the Confederate line crumbled, and victory fell upon the

Ohioans. However, it came at a great price: the 28th lost 2 officers and 26 men killed, and 110 men wounded. It was the largest number killed of any unit in Hunter's army. Later, some curious men counted the bullet and shrapnel holes in the regimental flag – they found 72.

On June 9, with enlistments expiring, the war-weary soldiers of the 28th Ohio went home. Receiving a hero's welcome upon their return to Cincinnati, most of the men officially mustered out of the army at Camp Dennison, Ohio, on July 23, 1864. However, over 220 men of the regiment re-enlisted into the 28th Ohio Infantry Battalion and served out the rest of the war performing guard duty in Wheeling, West Virginia.

Vernon Schmid

28th Ohio Volunteer Infantry
2nd German Regiment
Image courtesy of Ohio Historical Society

Service Assignments

2nd Brigade, Kanawha Division, Dept. of the Mountains, to September, 1862.

2nd Brigade, Kanawha Division, 9th Army Corps, Army of the Potomac, to October, 1862.

2nd Brigade, Kanawha Division, District of West Virginia, Dept. of the Ohio, to March, 1863.

Averill's 4th Separate Brigade, 8th Army Corps, Middle Department, to June, 1863.

Averill's 4th Separate Brigade, Dept. of West Virginia, to December, 1863.

1st Brigade, 4th Division, West Virginia, to April, 1864.
1st Brigade, 1st Infantry Division , West Virginia, to
June, 1864.

28ᵗʰ Ohio Regimental Colors
2ⁿᵈ German Regiment
Image Courtesy of Ohio Historical Society

Unit Service

- Moved from Point Pleasant, Va., to Clarksburg, August 11-12, 1861, thence to Buckhannon, August 17-19, to Bulltown August 28-29, to Sutton September 1 and to Summerville September 7-9.
- Battle of Carnifex Ferry, W. Va., September 10.
- March to Camp Lookout and Big Sewell Mountain September 15-23.
- Retreat to Camp Anderson October 6-9.
  Operations in the Kanawha Valley and New River Region October 19-November 17.
- New River October 19-21.
- Moved to Gauley December 6, and duty there till May, 1862.

- Advance on Virginia & Tennessee Railroad May 10.
- Princeton May 11-15-16 and 17.
- Wolf Creek May 15.
- Flat Top Mountain till August.
- Blue Stone August 13-14.
- Movement to Washington, D.C., August 15-24.
- Maryland Campaign September 6-22.
- Battles of Frederick City, Md., September 12.
- South Mountain September 14.
- Antietam September 16-17.
- March to Clear Springs October 8, thence to Hancock October 9.
- March to the Kanawha Valley, West Va., October 14-November 17.
- Duty at Brownstown November 17, 1862, to January 8, 1863.
- Scout to Boone, Wyoming and Logan Counties December 1-10, 1862.
- Moved to Buckhannon January 8, 1863, thence to Clarksburg April 26-27, and to Weston May 9-12.
- Moved to New Creek June 17, thence to Beverly July 2-7, and duty there till November 1.
- Averill's Raid from Beverly against Lewisburg and the Virginia & Tennessee Railroad November 1-17.
- Mill Point November 5.
- Droop Mountain November 6.
- Elk Mountain hear Hillsborough November 10.
- March through Elk Mountain Pass to Beverly December 13-17, and duty at Beverly till April 23, 1864.

- Moved to Join Army of the Shenandoah at Bunker Hill April 23-29.
- Sigel's Expedition to New Market April 30-May 16.
- Battle of New Market May 16.
- Hunter's Expedition to Lynchburg, Va., May 26-June 8.
- Piedmont June 5.
- Occupation of Staunton June 6.
- March to Webster on the Baltimore & Ohio Railroad with 1,000 prisoners, wounded and refugees, June 8-18.
- Guard prisoners to Camp Morton, Ind., thence moved to Cincinnati, Ohio.
- Mustered out June 23, 1864.
- Reorganized as a Veteran Battalion September, 1864, and ordered to Wheeling, W. Va., duty in the Reserve Division of West Virginia, till July, 1865.
- Mustered out at Wheeling, W. Va., July 13, 1865.
- Regiment lost during service 2 Officers and 66 Enlisted men killed and mortally wounded and 66 Enlisted men by disease. Total 134.

Vernon Schmid

.

Sources

Davis, William C. *The Battle of New Market* (Baton Rouge, Louisiana, 1975).

Ford Henry A. and Kate Ford, *History of Cincinnati, Ohio* (Cleveland, Ohio, 1881).

Hochbruch, Wolfgang. "Forty-Eighters" in the Union Armies: A Preliminary Checklist (Germany, 2001).

Hunt, Roger D. Hunt and Jack R. Brown. *Brevet Brigadier Generals in Blue* (Gaithersburg, Maryland, 1990).

Johnson, Robert U. and Clarence C. Buel, *Battles and Leaders of the Civil War*, vol. 1 (Secaucus, New Jersey, 1887).

Kennedy, Frances H. *The Civil War Battlefield Guide*, 2nd Edition (New York, 1998).

Lowry, Terry. *Last Sleep: The Battle of Droop Mountain November 6, 1863* (Charleston, West Virginia, 1996).

McPherson, James M. *For Cause and Comrades: Why Men fought in the Civil War* (New York, 1997).

Walker, Gary C. *Hunter's Fiery Raid Through Virginia Valleys* (Roanoke, Virginia, 1989).

Patchan, Scott C. *Forgotten Fury: The Battle of Piedmont, Va.* (Fredericksburg, Virginia, 1995).

Fox, William F. *Regimental Losses in the American Civil War (1861-1865)* (Albany, New York, 1889).

Dyer, Frederick H. Dyer, *A Compendium of the War of the Rebellion*, vol. 3 (New York, 1959).

Davis, Major George B. and Perry, Leslie J. *The Official Military Atlas of the Civil War*. New York, 1983.

Dyer, Frederick H. A Compendium of the War of the Rebellion. Vol. 3. New York, 1959.

Ford, Henry A. and Ford, Kate. History of Cincinnati, Ohio. Cleveland, Ohio, 1881.

_____. History of Hamilton County, Ohio. Cleveland, Ohio, 1881.

Fox, William F. *Regimental Losses in the American Civil War (1861-1865)*. Albany, New York, 1889.

Priest, John Michael. *Before Antietam: The Battle for South Mountain* (Oxford, 1992).

_____. *Antietam: The Soldiers' Battle* (Oxford, 1989).

Reid, Whitelaw. *Ohio in the War. Vol. 2.* (Cincinnati, Ohio, 1868).

Roster Commission of Ohio. Official Roster of the Soldiers of the State of Ohio in the War of the Rebellion – 1861-1866. Vol. 3. Cincinnati, Ohio, 1888.

Warner, Ezra J. *Generals in Blue: Lives of the*

Union Commanders. Baton Rouge, Louisiana, 1992.

Williams, C.S. *Williams' Cincinnati Directory, City Guide & Business Mirror* (Cincinnati, Ohio, 1861).

Wimberg, Robert J. *Cincinnati and the Civil War: Off to Battle*. Cincinnati, 1992.

_____. *Cincinnati and the Civil War: Under Attack*. Cincinnati, 1992.

United States Census Bureau. Seventh Census of the United States, 1850, Cincinnati, Hamilton County, Ohio.

_____. Eighth Census of the United States, 1860, Cincinnati, Hamilton County, Ohio.

_____. Ninth Census of the United States, 1870, Cincinnati, Hamilton County, Ohio.

_____. Tenth Census of the United States, 1880, Cincinnati, Hamilton County, Ohio.

United States Quartermaster's Department, Roll of Honor: Names of Soldiers Who Died in the Defense of the American Union Interred in the National Cemeteries (Baltimore, Maryland, 1995).

United States War Department. War of the Rebellion: Official Records of the Union and Confederate Armies. 128 vols. Washington, D.C., 1880-1901.

Made in the USA
Las Vegas, NV
16 March 2022

45750867R00025